Johnsto

by Jeffrey M

Lang**Syne**

PUBLISHING
WRITING *to* REMEMBER

Lang**Syne**

PUBLISHING

WRITING *to* REMEMBER

79 Main Street, Newtongrange,
Midlothian EH22 4NA
Tel: 0131 344 0414   Fax: 0845 075 6085
E-mail: info@lang-syne.co.uk
www.langsyneshop.co.uk

Design by Dorothy Meikle
Printed by Ricoh Print Scotland
© Lang Syne Publishers Ltd 2015

ISBN 978-1-85217-097-4

Johnstone

*"The spirit of the clan means much
to thousands of people"*

The origins of the clan system

by Rennie McOwan

The original Scottish clans of the Highlands and the great families of the Lowlands and Borders were gatherings of families, relatives, allies and neighbours for mutual protection against rivals or invaders.

Scotland experienced invasion from the Vikings, the Romans and English armies from the south. The Norman invasion of what is now England also had an influence on land-holding in Scotland. Some of these invaders stayed on and in time became 'Scottish'.

The word clan derives from the Gaelic language term 'clann', meaning children, and it was first used many centuries ago as communities were formed around tribal lands in glens and mountain fastnesses.

The format of clans changed over the centuries, but at its best the chief and his family held the land on behalf of all, like trustees, and the ordinary clansmen and women believed they had a blood relationship with the founder of their clan.

There were two way duties and obligations. An inadequate chief could be deposed and replaced by someone of greater ability.

Clan people had an immense pride in race. Their relationship with the chief was like adult children to a father and they had a real dignity.

The concept of clanship is very old and a more feudal notion of authority gradually crept in.

Pictland, for instance, was divided into seven principalities ruled by feudal leaders who were the strongest and most charismatic leaders of their particular groups.

By the sixth century the 'British' kingdoms of Strathclyde, Lothian and Celtic Dalriada (Argyll) had emerged and Scotland, as one nation, began to take shape in the time of King Kenneth MacAlpin.

Some chiefs claimed descent from ancient kings which may not have been accurate in every case.

By the twelfth and thirteenth centuries the clans and families were more strongly brought under the central control of Scottish monarchs.

Lands were awarded and administered more and more under royal favour, yet the power of the area clan chiefs was still very great.

The long wars to ensure Scotland's independence against the expansionist ideas of English monarchs extended the influence of some clans and reduced the lands of others.

Those who supported Scotland's greatest king, Robert the Bruce, were awarded the territories of the families who had opposed his claim to the Scottish throne.

In the Scottish Borders country – the notorious Debatable Lands – the great families built up a ferocious reputation for providing warlike men accustomed to raiding into England and occasionally fighting one another.

Chiefs had the power to dispense justice and to confiscate lands and clan warfare produced a society where martial virtues – courage, hardiness, tenacity – were greatly admired.

Gradually the relationship between the clans and the Crown became strained as Scottish monarchs became more orientated to life in the Lowlands and, on occasion, towards England.

The Highland clans spoke a different language, Gaelic, whereas the language of Lowland Scotland and the court was Scots and in more modern times, English.

Highlanders dressed differently, had different

customs, and their wild mountain land sometimes seemed almost foreign to people living in the Lowlands.

It must be emphasised that Gaelic culture was very rich and story-telling, poetry, piping, the clarsach (harp) and other music all flourished and were greatly respected.

Highland culture was different from other parts of Scotland but it was not inferior or less sophisticated.

Central Government, whether in London or Edinburgh, sometimes saw the Gaelic clans as a challenge to their authority and some sent expeditions into the Highlands and west to crush the power of the Lords of the Isles.

Nevertheless, when the eighteenth century Jacobite Risings came along the cause of the Stuarts was mainly supported by Highland clans.

The word Jacobite comes from the Latin for James – Jacobus. The Jacobites wanted to restore the exiled Stuarts to the throne of Britain.

The monarchies of Scotland and England became one in 1603 when King James VI of Scotland (1st of England) gained the English throne after Queen Elizabeth died.

The Union of Parliaments of Scotland and England, the Treaty of Union, took place in 1707.

Some Highland clans, of course, and Lowland families opposed the Jacobites and supported the incoming Hanoverians.

After the Jacobite cause finally went down at Culloden in 1746 a kind of ethnic cleansing took place. The power of the chiefs was curtailed. Tartan and the pipes were banned in law.

Many emigrated, some because they wanted to, some because they were evicted by force. In addition, many Highlanders left for the cities of the south to seek work.

Many of the clan lands became home to sheep and deer shooting estates.

But the warlike traditions of the clans and the great Lowland and Border families lived on, with their descendants fighting bravely for freedom in two world wars.

Remember the men from whence you came, says the Gaelic proverb, and to that could be added the role of many heroic women.

The spirit of the clan, of having roots, whether Highland or Lowland, means much to thousands of people.

Name's the Same

Johnstone and Johnston are two alternate spellings of the same name. Many persons who spell their surname Johnson also share the same heritage. According to Dr. George F. Black, in former times the name was spelled in many other ways, including Jhonestown (1609), Jhonstoun (1616), Johanstoun (1450), Johnestoun (1493), Johngston (1736), Johnnesonne (1530), Johnnestoun (1608), Johnnestoune (1558), Johnnstoun (1503), Johnstounne (1575), Joneston (1245), Jonhesone (1491), Jonhstone (1499), Joniston (1329) and Jonstoun (1683). The name is of Anglo-Saxon derivation and means "John's settlement".

The largest group of Johnstones is from Dumfriesshire near the English border in southwestern Scotland. There are also Johnstones from Aberdeenshire in northeastern Scotland, and Johnstones who took their name from the former name of Perth (St. Johnstoun) or various other places once called Johnston or Johnstone, such as Jonystoun (now Johnstonburn) in the parish of Humbie, East Lothian.

Today, all Johnstones are considered to be members of a single clan.

Tartan and Badge

Tartan: The Johnstone tartan appeared in the *Vestiarium Scoticum*, a book published in 1842 by two brothers who claimed to be grandsons of Bonnie Prince Charlie. The *Vestiarium Scoticum* purported to be a copy of an ancient manuscript detailing the tartans of the various clans, but modern examination has shown it to be a forgery. Nonetheless, many tartans that are revered today had their origins in this work.

Crest Badge: In the modern Scottish tradition, the Johnstone crest badge consists of the Chief's crest (a winged spur) enclosed in a conventional representation of a strap and buckle, upon which is inscribed the Chief's motto, *Nunquam Non Paratus*, which is Latin for "Never Unprepared".

Red hawthorn is the plant badge of the Clan. This is probably an invention of the nineteenth century. Border clans did not use plant badges, which were characteristic of highland clans.

The original war cry or slogan of Clan Johnstone was "Light Thieves All", which was a demand to the enemy to dismount and surrender. This slogan was also used as the first motto in the Chief's armorial bearings in the early seventeenth century. Later, the Chief adopted the current motto, *Nunquam Non Paratus*. Sometimes the Chief's motto is translated as "Ready, Aye Ready" or simply "Aye Ready".

The Border Clan

Many peoples contributed to the ethnic composition of the Scottish Borderers, including Picts, ancient British tribes who spoke a Celtic language akin to Welsh, soldiers from the four corners of the Roman Empire, Gaelic Scots, Angles from Northumbria, Vikings, and Normans. Borderers were not typical Scottish "lowlanders". Until the early seventeenth century, they maintained a very distinctive society of their own.

The Borderers were the product of a brutal frontier. Centuries of border warfare with England after the Scottish War of Independence had discouraged crop farming. Instead, the Borderers became restless and mobile, raiding the English and neighbouring Scots to replenish the cattle and horses that constituted their principal form of property. They were excellent horsemen. Dressed in a metal helmet (steel bonnet), reinforced leather jacket (jack) and high riding boots, with a long lance, cutting sword, and set of pistols, a Borderer was well adapted to his world. A monument at the Devil's Beeftub, a vast, sinister-looking hollow near the source of the Annan River, records that the Johnstones used the place "to hide cattle stolen in predatory raids".

For administrative and military purposes, the border was divided into three Scottish regions, and three English ones, called "Marches". Each March was controlled by a March Warden appointed by the king of Scotland or England. Eastern Dumfriesshire, the primary Johnstone region, was in the Scottish West March.

Like the Highlands, the Borders were remote and hilly. Although feudalism existed, tribal loyalty was much more important. Border life consisted of a warrior society that had much in common with Highland life, including clanship. However, Borderers did not wear tartan or Highland dress. In language and culture, historically they were much closer to the Scots of the central Lowlands than to those of the Highlands or Isles.

Like many warrior societies, the Scottish Borderers created epic poetry. The Border Ballads vividly express a brutal, tragic, and yet heroic way of life. Several well-known examples, particularly *The*

Lads of Wamphray and *Lord Maxwell's Last Goodnight*, concern events in Johnstone history.

Border lairds lived in stark, stone peel towers, three or four stories tall, surmounted with battlements and built on inaccessible ground. An outer stone wall called a "barmkin" surrounded the tower and adjacent outbuildings. Some clansmen lived in fortified farmhouses called "bastle houses".

In 1587, the Parliament of Scotland passed a law "for the quieting and keeping in obedience of the disorderly subject inhabitants of the borders, highlands and isles". Attached to the law was a Roll of the Clans that contained both Borders and Highland portions. The Borders part of the Roll listed the Johnstones as a clan with a chief in the Scottish West March. Thus, it is historically correct to refer to the Johnstones as a clan. Since the Borderers were great horsemen, the clans of the Borders are sometimes called the "riding clans". They are sometimes referred to as "Names". Branches of clans were sometimes called "graynes".

It is improbable that most members of any border clan actually descended in the male line from a single progenitor. More likely, people in a particular geographic area gave their allegiance to the local warlord, took his name, and came to accept his ancestry as their own. For example, not all Johnstones are from the same origin. However, intermarriage over time no doubt resulted in many clansmen being related to the Chief, and to each other, on either the paternal or maternal side.

For a long time, the Scots of Edinburgh and the central Lowlands treated Borderers as pariahs and did not even think of them as fellow countrymen. A law of 1587 actually expelled Borderers from the inland counties of Scotland unless they could find security for their quiet deportment. The Borderers felt the same way about the inland Scots. Since the borderers' experience with their kings was more often that of royal vengeance than protection, the Borderers referred to the Scottish monarchs as "kings of Fife and Lothian", districts in which the Borderers were not allowed to settle. In fact, Scottish and English Borderers had much more in common with each other than they had with the inland inhabitants of their respective countries.

When King James VI of Scotland succeeded to the English throne in 1603, the border frontier became the centre of a new and united kingdom. The king used his new authority to deal with the unruly border clansmen as ruthlessly as his successors confronted the Highland clans a century and a half later. A proclamation of 1605 forbade Borderers, "except nobles and gentlemen unsuspected of felony or theft", from carrying "jacks, spears, lances, swords, daggers, steel caps, hackbuts, pistols, platesleaves, and suchlike". It also forbade the owning of any horse above the value of 50 shillings sterling or 30 pounds Scots. The government deported or executed the worst of the troublemakers, including many Johnstones. The old border frontier ceased to exist within a few short years.

Origins and History

The Johnstones are first identified by name shortly after the time when King David I of Scotland (1124-1153) induced many Norman knights from England to settle north of the border. The first known Johnstone was Gilbert, son of John, who received the use of a small amount of land in Warmanby and Annan in southern Annandale from William Bruce, the Norman Lord of Annandale, between 1195 and 1214. Soon, Gilbert was knighted and witnessed various charters as Sir Gilbert de Joneston. Later Johnstone lairds fought the English at the Battle of Solway in 1378 and the Battle of Otterbourne in 1388.

The Johnstones were among the most intrepid reivers of the Scottish West March. They rose to power by assisting the king in crushing the Douglas rebellion in 1455. The Black Douglases virtually controlled southern Scotland and were perceived as a serious threat to the Stewart dynasty. The Johnstones fought the Black Douglases at Arkinholm in Dumfriesshire and participated in the king's siege of Threave Castle in Kirkudbright. Finally, the king stripped the Black Douglases of their titles and confiscated their estates. King James II rewarded his supporters, including the Johnstones, with grants of former Douglas lands. Johnstone clansmen soon spread throughout upper Annandale and into Lanarkshire.

The principal stronghold of the Johnstones was Lochwood Castle, a massive fortress having an L-shaped tower that was surrounded by forest and marsh. On approaching Lochwood, King James V is said to have remarked "He who built it must have been a knave in his heart". The first known reference to the stone castle of Lochwood, by name, was in November 1476, in a Latin document in which John Johnstone of that Ilk (Johannes Johnnestoune de eodem) conveyed the lands of Wamphray to his son John. The document was written and signed at "Lochwod"[sic]. In 1542,

Queen Mary of Guise designated the lands of the Laird of Johnstone a free barony. Lochwood is considered the seat of the Johnstone clan. The Chief's family still holds the Free Barony granted in 1542 and a host of others.

The English soldier Thomas Carelton captured Lochwood by stealth in 1547 while the Laird of Johnstone was a prisoner in England. Several of his English soldiers scaled Lochwood's barmkin, or outer wall, during the night and hid until daylight. They gained entrance to the castle when a woman inside opened the iron "yett", or gate, at dawn. The English held Lochwood until 1550 and burned it as they left.

Feud with the Maxwells

During the sixteenth century, the Johnstones and the Maxwells competed for primacy in the Scottish West March. Johnstone and Maxwell chiefs each served at various times as wardens. Their respective followers continued a deadly blood feud for almost a century.

Robert Maxwell, brother of Lord Maxwell, led a force of 400 horsemen to Annandale, land of the Johnstones, in April 1585. He burned Lochwood so that, in his words "Lady Johnstone might have light to put on her hood". The Johnstone family charter chest was destroyed in the fire.

Later, Johnstone reivers slew a number of Crichtons of Sanquhar. The widows of the slaughtered men waved the bloody shirts of the slain in the streets of Edinburgh and protested for retribution.

In late 1593, John, seventh Lord Maxwell, Earl of Morton, sometime collaborator with the Spanish Armada and Warden of the Scottish West March, assembled 2,000 armed horsemen and, displaying the king's banner, invaded the district of Annandale. Whatever the official reason, Lord Maxwell's personal intention was to destroy his family's ancient enemies and rivals for power in southwestern Scotland, once and for all.

Sir James Johnstone of Dunskellie, Chief of the Johnstones, received advance warning of the approaching army and realized that his clan would soon have a desperate fight for continued existence. He summoned help from Grahams, Scotts, Carrutherses, Irvings, Elliots and others, and quickly raised a force of about 800. Among those who aided the clan was the Chief's eleven-year-old kinsman, Robert Johnstone of Raecleuch. Lord Maxwell had offered his followers a reward for the head or hand of the Laird of Johnstone, and Sir James in turn offered his followers a reward for the head or hand of Lord Maxwell.

On December 6, 1593, the Maxwell army approached the Johnstone town of Lockerbie near a riverbank called Dryfe Sands. Sir James kept most of his men hidden, but sent a handful of horsemen to provoke the Maxwell vanguard, then retreat. When the vanguard broke ranks in pursuit with loud cries of victory, the main body of Johnstones made a sudden, desperate charge, catching the Maxwells off guard and driving the disorganized vanguard into the main force. The Johnstone horsemen then pursued their enemies through the streets of Lockerbie and into the Water of Dryfe, slaughtering some 700 of the Maxwells and their followers, and slashing the heads of dismounted foes with downward sword or axe strokes that caused gruesome facial wounds known as "Lockerbie licks".

In the midst of the carnage, Lord Maxwell begged for mercy and offered to surrender, but the Johnstones cut off his outstretched arm and slew him. It is said that the Laird of Johnstone affixed the head and right hand of Lord Maxwell to the battlements of Lochwood Castle as bloody trophies of the Johnstones' overwhelming victory at the Battle of Dryfe Sands.

In 1608, a meeting was arranged for a reconciliation of Sir James Johnstone of Dunskellie and Lord Maxwell, son of the chief who was killed at the

Battle of Dryfe Sands. Precautions were taken for
each party to bring only one attendant. During the
interview, Lord Maxwell suddenly drew a pistol from
under his cloak and shot the Johnstone Chief in the
back with two poisoned bullets, mortally wounding
him. After escaping to France, Lord Maxwell eventually returned to Scotland, thinking all would be forgiven. However, all was not forgiven and he was
apprehended. In 1613 Lord Maxwell was publicly
beheaded in Edinburgh for his "murder under trust" of
Sir James Johnstone of Dunskellie.

Another decade passed before the feud finally
terminated. At the instance of King James VI, in 1623
the two chiefs, Robert, Earl of Nithsdale, Lord
Maxwell, and James Johnstone of Johnstone, finally
met and "choppit hands" in Edinburgh before the Privy
Council, as a formal public gesture of reconciliation.

The Chief's Family

In 1633, at the coronation of King Charles I in
Scotland, James Johnstone, son of Sir James
Johnstone of Dunskellie, was created a first lord of
Parliament with the designation of Lord Johnstone of
Lochwood. In 1643 he became Earl of Hartfell, Lord
Johnstone of Lochwood, Moffatdale and Evandale.

During the religious wars, the Earl joined the Covenanters, but later he supported the royalist cause under Montrose. The Covenanter army captured the Earl at Philliphaugh near Selkirk in 1645 and condemned him to death, but later commuted the punishment to a fine of 100,000 pounds Scots. During the Commonwealth, the Earl of Hartfell and his son were imprisoned in Edinburgh, Dumbarton and St. Andrews castles. Upon the Restoration, King Charles II rewarded James, the second Earl of Hartfell, for loyalty with Letters Patent to the Earldom of Annandale, a peerage formerly held by the Murray family, but which had become vacant and available for reissue.

The destination of the 1661 Letters Patent was to heirs male and then to heirs female. Since the Earl had only daughters at the time, he feared that the title could pass to heirs male who were distant relatives, to the exclusion of his own descendants. For this reason, the Earl tried to change the destination of the peerage so that it would pass to his female descendants, if he had no male ones. In 1662 the Earl obtained a Crown Charter that re-granted the same peerage with the desired destination, so that it would pass to the Earl's female descendants before passing to distantly-related male heirs. This Crown Charter created a second Earldom of Annandale, without superseding the original title.

William Johnstone, the second Earl of Annandale, participated in a Jacobite plot as a youth but eventually regained the favour of King William I and became an Extraordinary Lord of Session, Lord of the Treasury, Lord of the Privy Counsel, Knight of the Thistle, Joint Secretary of State for Scotland, Keeper of the Great Seal, and Privy Counselor. In 1701, the King made him Marquis of Annandale in recognition of his service.

William's oldest surviving son, James, the second Marquis of Annandale, died unmarried in 1730, in Naples. The first Marquis's posthumous son, George, was the third Marquis, and when he died unmarried in 1792 the titles became dormant.

In 1983, after a lapse of nearly two centuries, the Lord Lyon King of Arms officially recognized Major Percy Wentworth Hope Johnstone of Annandale and of that Ilk, hereditary Keeper of Lochmaben Castle and a descendant of the daughter of the first Marquis of Annandale, as Chief of Clan Johnstone. Upon Major Hope Johnstone's death later that year, his son Patrick Andrew Wentworth Hope Johnstone succeeded as Chief.

In 1985 the House of Lords recognized the Chief's claim to the long-dormant titles of Earl of Annandale and Hartfell under the Crown Charter of 1662. The original Earldom granted under the 1661 Letters Patent still awaits a qualified claimant who can prove he is an heir male of the first Earl of Annandale. If that were to happen, it is possible that there could be two separate Earls of Annandale.

The Chief resides with his wife, Lady Annandale, at Annanbank, Dumfriesshire.

Various Branches

In 1578 the "nayme of Johnnstounis" appointed a council of twelve arbiters to settle internal disputes, all under the leadership of their "chief and maister" the Laird of Johnstone. The council consisted of Johnstones of Carnsalloch, Craigieburn, Elsieshields, Fairholm, Fingland, Howgill, Lockerbie, Marjoribanks, Millbank, Newton, Poldean, and Wamphray. During the sixteenth century, the clan was also organized in numerous "gangs", which changed form over time. Following are descriptions of some of the major branches.

The Lockerbie Johnstones

The Johnstones of Lockerbie in Dryfesdale Parish are said to be of the same stock as the Johnstones of Elsieshields in nearby Lochmaben Parish. This is perhaps the largest group of Johnstones, and it may include some of the Johnstones in surrounding parishes, such as the Johnstones of Millbank in Applegarth Parish, the Fingland Johnstones in Wamphray Parish, and the Johnstones of Tundergarth. The heiress of the main family of Lockerbie Johnstones married into a family of Douglases to become the Johnstone-Douglas family of Lockerbie.

The Wamphray Johnstones

The Johnstones of Wamphray Parish consisted of descendants of the Chief, the Wamphray Johnstones, and other Johnstones such as the Poldean and Fingland Johnstones. The Old Gang of Wamphray was famous as a fearsome group of reivers. From the Poldean Johnstones descend the Johnstones of Corehead, Craigieburn, and others. Some Craigieburn Johnstones migrated to Poland and Germany.

The Westerhall Johnstones

The Johnstones of Westerhall may be an early

offshoot of the Annandale Johnstones. They claim that the first member of the family, Matthew Johnstone, was a son of the Chief of the Johnstones, and that he received from the King land called Westraw in Pettinain Parish, Lanarkshire, for service in the Battle of Arkinholm in 1455. History records that the king rewarded the Johnstones with land for their role at Arkinholm, but it has never been proven conclusively that Matthew Johnstone, founder of the Westraw (later Westerhall) branch, was a son of the Chief of the Johnstones.

Around the beginning of the seventeenth century, the Johnstones of Westraw sold their land in Lanarkshire and purchased an estate in the parish of Westerkirk, Dumfriesshire, not far from the site of the Battle of Arkinholm. They named their new estate Westerhall and henceforth have been known as Johnstones of Westerhall. The family prospered and in 1700 Sir John Johnstone of Westerhall was created a baronet of Nova Scotia. Many representatives of the family served as Members of Parliament, for Dumfries and other seats. Lord Derwent of Hackness Hall in Scarborough, North Yorkshire, is descended from the second son of the second Baronet of Westerhall.

The Gretna and Newbie Johnstones

The Gretna Johnstones might be descended from the Johnstones of Annandale, but this has not been proven. The Gretna Johnstones lived in south Annandale, by the Solway Firth. In 1541, William Johnstone of Gretna obtained a charter erecting Newbie Castle and the surrounding estate into a Barony. Newbie passed to Sir James Johnstone of Dunskellie, the Chief, in 1607. From the Johnstones of Gretna and Newbie descend the Johnstones of Galabank and Fulford Hall.

Johnstones in Edinburgh

Beginning in the sixteenth century, Johnstones began relocating to Edinburgh. Some of these Johnstones were descended from the Elsieshields, Poldean and Bierholm Johnstones. Among the descendants of Eslsieshields were the Kellobank Johnstones. From Bierholm descended the Johnstones of Warriston, Sheens and Hilton. The Hilton Johnstones later spread into Berwickshire in the east Borders.

The Caskieben Johnstons

Stephen de Johnston, who lived during the reign of King David II (1329-71), was the progenitor of the Johnstons of Caskieben in Aberdeenshire. Stephen is said to have been a brother of the Laird of Johnstone in Annandale, but this has never been proven. He was a learned man who retired to the north from troubles in his own country and became principal secretary to Thomas, Earl of Mar. Stephen de Johnston married Margaret, daughter and heiress of Sir Andrew Garrioch of Caskieben, with whom he received a considerable estate in Aberdeenshire, including the lands of Caskieben, Crimond, Cordyce, and others. He also received the lands of Kinbrown, which he called Johnston, after his own name.

Stephen de Johnston and Margaret Garrioch had a son named John Johnston of Caskieben, who succeeded his father and who was also proprietor of the lands of Ballindallach. John's son Gilbert de Johnston was designated by the title of Ballindalloch during his father's lifetime. Gilbert was succeeded by his eldest son, Alexander, who had his lands of Caskieben designated a free barony, called Johnston, during the reign of King James II (1437-60). Another son, William, received the lands of Ballindalloch and from him descend the Johnstons of Crimond.

William Johnston, eldest son of Alexander, was killed at the Battle of Flodden in 1513. The

Johnstons of Cayesmill are descended from Alexander's second son. A later William Johnston, younger of Caskieben, was slain at the Battle of Pinkie in 1547, during the lifetime of his father.

Sir George Johnston of Caskieben mortgaged all of his properties when he was 23 years old. In 1633, when he could not repay the debt, his properties passed to Alexander Jaffray. In 1662, Sir John Keith acquired the castle of Caskieben, enlarged it, and renamed it Keith Hall. Sir George was made a Baronet of Nova Scotia in 1626. He also became Sheriff of Aberdeen in 1630.

Sir John Johnston of Caskieben, third Baronet, was a captain in the army, and served in Flanders and at the Battle of the Boyne. He was involved with Captain James Campbell, who abducted and forcibly married a thirteen-year-old heiress named Mary Wharton. Miss Wharton's relative, Lord Wharton, obtained a proclamation from King William offering a reward for the capture of Campbell and Johnston. Campbell escaped to Scotland. However, Johnston's landlord betrayed him for 50 pounds. Johnston was tried at the Old Bailey and was executed in December 1690.

In 1700, John Johnston, fourth Baronet, changed the name of his estate of Newplace to

"Caskieben", but he lost the property to his creditors in 1707. Later, he led his followers in the Jacobite cause to defeat at the Battle of Sheriffmuir in 1715, where his only son was killed.

The current head of the Caskieben branch is Sir Thomas Alexander Johnston of Caskieben, 14th Baronet, an American citizen.

Johnstones in Northern Ireland

After 1603, the Crown deported a number of Johnstones and other unruly Borderers to Northern Ireland in connection with the pacification of the Borders. Many Johnstones also went to the Ulster Plantation voluntarily. Soon, Johnstones became numerous throughout Northern Ireland. Many of the Ulster Johnstones ultimately emigrated to North America, where they continued the frontier tradition.

References:

Black, George F. *The Surnames of Scotland, their Origin, Meaning and History.* New York: New York Public Library, 1946.

Dewar, Peter Beauclerk, ed. *Burke's Landed Gentry the Kingdom in Scotland.* Boydell & Brewer Inc., 2001.

Fraser, George MacDonald. *The Steel Bonnets.* London: Pan Books, 1974.

Fraser, Sir William. *The Annandale Family Book of the Johnstones, Earls and Marquises of Annandale.* 2 vols. Edinburgh, n.p., 1894.

Fraser, Sir William. *The Book of Carlaverock.* 2 vols. Edinburgh, n.p., 1873.

Great Britain. Edinburgh. H.M. General Register House. *Register of the Privy Council of Scotland,* 1877.

Great Britain. Historical Manuscripts Commission. *The Manuscripts of J.J. Hope Johnstone of Annandale.* London: Eyre and Spottiswoode, 1897.

Honey, Russell C. *The "Gentle" Johnston/es, The Story of the Johnston/e Family.* Ameliasburgh Township: Fallsbrook Publishing, Inc., 1996.

Johnstone, C.L. *History of the Johnstones.* Edinburgh: W.& A.K. Johnston, [1909].

Johnstone, C.L. *The Historical Families of Dumfriesshire and the Border Wars.* Second Edition. Bowie: Heritage Books, Inc., 1994.

Kermack, W.R. *The Scottish Borders (with Galloway) to 1603.* Edinburgh: Johnston & Bacon, 1967.

Mackie, J.D. *A History of Scotland.* 2nd ed. Harmondsworth, Middlesex: Penguin Books Ltd., 1985.

Merriman, Marcus. "The Platte of Castlemilk, 1547", *Dumfriesshire and Galloway Natural History & Antiquarian Society - Transactions,* Third Series, Vol. XLIV, pp. 175-181, 1967.

Marsden, John. *The Illustrated Border Ballads.* Austin: University of Texas Press, 1990.

Maxwell-Irving, Alastair M.T. "Lochwood Castle - A Prelininary Site Survey", *Dumfriesshire and Galloway Natural History & Antiquarian Society - Transactions,* Third Series, Vol. XLV, pp. 184-199, 1968.

Maxwell-Irving, Alastair M.T. "Lochwood Castle II - Exploratory

Excavations and Observations on Lochwood & Its Lairds" (unpublished), 1977.

Maxwell-Irving, Alastair M.T. "Lochwood Castle - A Resume", *Dumfriesshire and Galloway Natural History & Antiquarian Society - Transactions*, Third Series, Vol. LXV, pp. 93-99, 1990.

Maxwell-Irving, Alastair M.T. *The Border Towers of Scotland: Their History and Architecture - The West March*. Blairlogie, Stirlingshire: A.M.T. Maxwell-Irving, 2000.

McDowall, William. *History of the Burgh of Dumfries*. 4th ed. Dumfries: T.C. Farries & Co. Limited, [1985].

Pitcairn, Robert. *Criminal Trials in Scotland*. 3 vols. Edinburgh, n.p., 1833.

Reid, R.C. "Lochwood Tower", *Dumfriesshire and Galloway Natural History & Antiquarian Society - Transactions*, Third Series, Vol. XIII, pp. 187-193, 1925.

Salter, Mike. *Discovering Scottish Castles*. Aylbury, Bucks: Shire Publications Ltd., 1985.

Scott, Sir Walter. *Minstrelsy of the Scottish Border*, in *The Complete Works of Sir Walter Scott*. Vol. I. 7 vols. New York: Conner and Cooke, 1833.

Scott, Sir Walter. *The Border Antiquities of England and Scotland*. 2 vols. London: Longman, Hurst, Rees, Orme and Brown; J. Murray; John Greig; Constable and Co., 1814, 1817.

Shannon, Robert A. "The Origin of the Johnston Family in Dumfriesshire" (unpublished), 1985. Dumfriesshire.

Smout, T.C. *A History of the Scottish People 1560-1830*. London: Fontana Press, 1998.

Tabraham, Christopher J. "The Scottish Medieval Tower House as Lordly Residence in the Light of Recent Excavation", *Proceedings of the Society of Antiquaries of Scotland*, Vol. 118, p. 267, 1988.

Thomson, T., ed. *Acts of the Parliaments of Scotland*. Vol. III. Edinburgh: n.p., 1814.

Turnbull, W. Robertson. *History of Moffat: with Frequent Notices of Moffatdale and Annandale*. Edinburgh: W.P. Nimmo, 1871.

Warner, Gerald. *Homelands of the Clans*. London: Collins, 1980.

Watson, Godfrey. *The Border Reivers*. Warkworth: Sandhill Press, 1998.